Our Bodies

Our Lungs

Charlotte Guillain

Heinemann Library
Chicago, Illinois

www.heinemannraintree.com
Visit our website to find out
more information about
Heinemann-Raintree books.

To order:

☎ Phone 888-454-2279

💻 Visit www.heinemannraintree.com
to browse our catalog and order online.

Editorial: Rebecca Rissman, Laura Knowles, Nancy Dickmann,
 and Sian Smith
Picture research: Ruth Blair and Mica Brancic
Designed by Joanna Hinton-Malivoire
Original Illustrations © Capstone Global Library Ltd. 2010
Illustrated by Tony Wilson
Printed and bound by Leo Paper Group

14 13 12 11 10
10 9 8 7 6 5 4 3 2 1

Library of Congress Cataloging-in-Publication Data

Guillain, Charlotte.
 Our lungs / Charlotte Guillain.
   p. cm. -- (Our bodies)
 Includes bibliographical references and index.
 ISBN 978-1-4329-3594-8 (hc) -- ISBN 978-1-4329-3603-7 (pb)
1. Lungs--Juvenile literature. I. Title.
 QP121.G85 2010
 612.2--dc22
                         2009022298

Acknowledgments
The author and publisher are grateful to the following for
permission to reproduce copyright material:
Corbis pp.**4**, **22** (© John Fortunato Photography), **16**, **23** (©
moodboard), **17** (© Image Source), **18** (© Sven Hagolani/zefa);
iStockphoto pp.**8**, **9**, **20**; Photolibrary pp.**5** (© Image Source), **15**, **23**
(© Goodshoot), **19** (© Flirt Collection); Science Photo Library pp.**12** (©
Eye Of Science), **13**, **23** (© Martin Dohrn/ Royal College of Surgeons),
14 (© Coneyl Jay), **21** (© Ian Hooton).

Front cover photograph of a brother and sister playing football
reproduced with permission of Corbis (© HBSS). Back cover
photograph reproduced with permission of Photolibrary (©
Goodshoot).

Every effort has been made to contact copyright holders of any
material reproduced in this book. Any omissions will be rectified in
subsequent printings if notice is given to the publisher.

Contents

Body Parts

Our bodies have many parts.

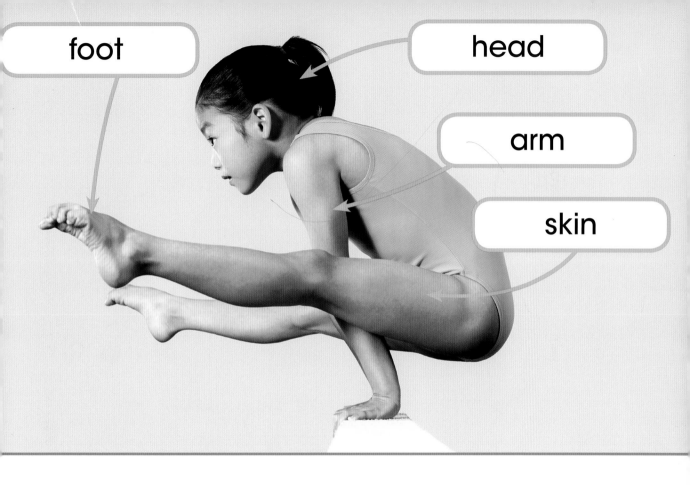

foot

head

arm

skin

Our bodies have parts on
the outside.

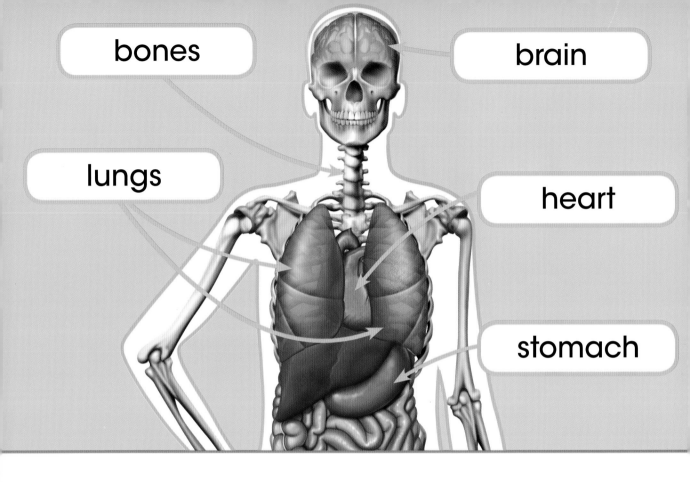

bones

brain

lungs

heart

stomach

Our bodies have parts on the inside.

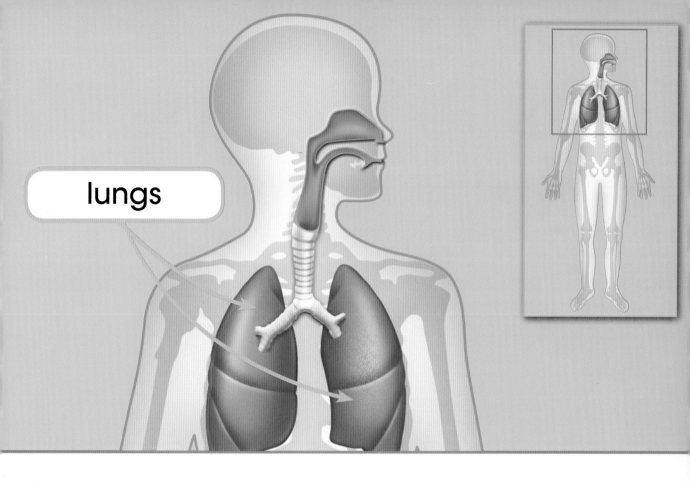

lungs

Your lungs are inside your body.

Your Lungs

You cannot see your lungs.

chest

Your lungs are inside your chest.

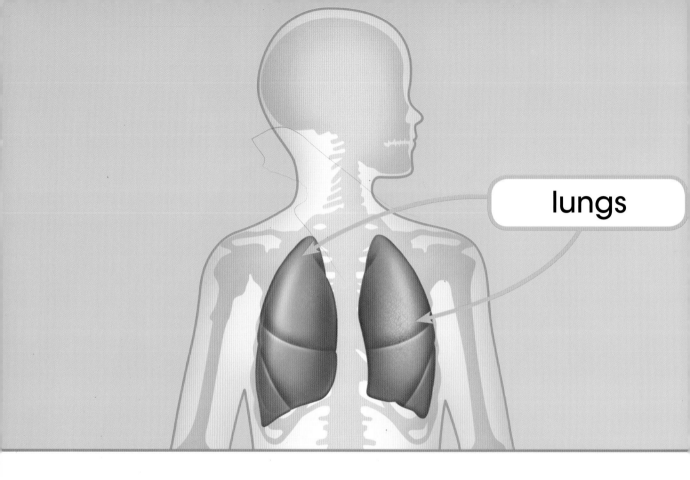

You have two lungs in your chest.

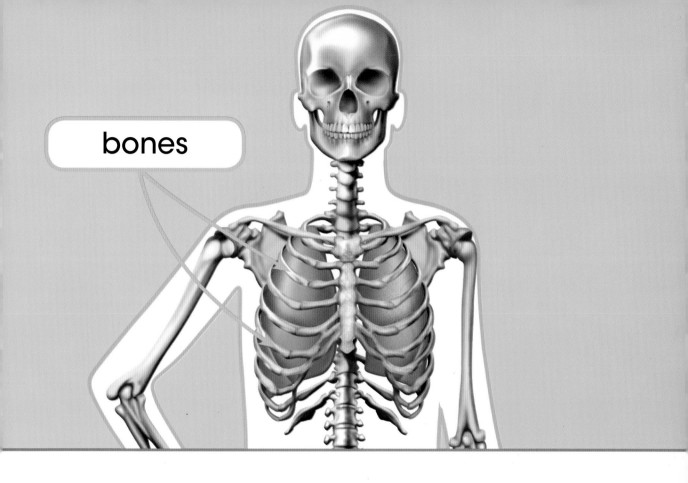

bones

Your bones keep your lungs safe.

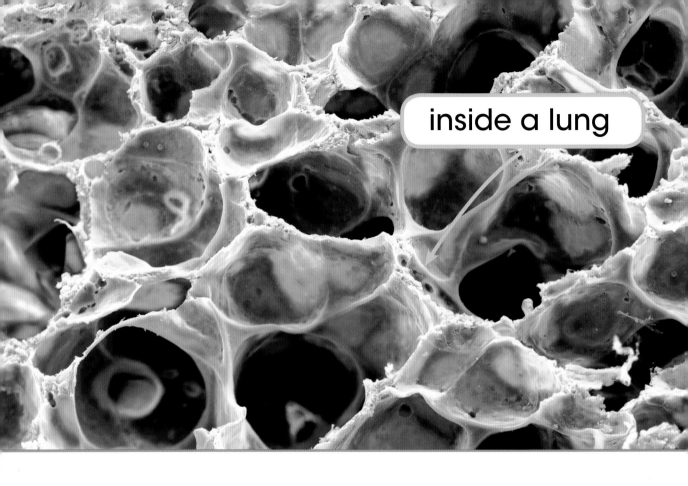

inside a lung

Your lungs are soft, like a sponge.

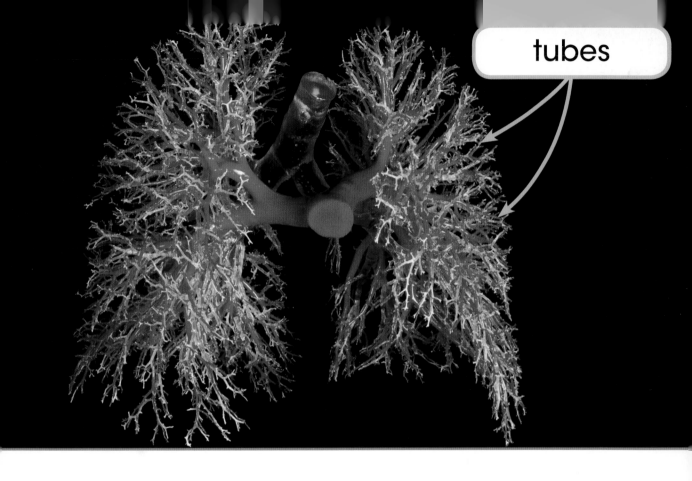

tubes

Your lungs are full of tiny tubes.

Breathing

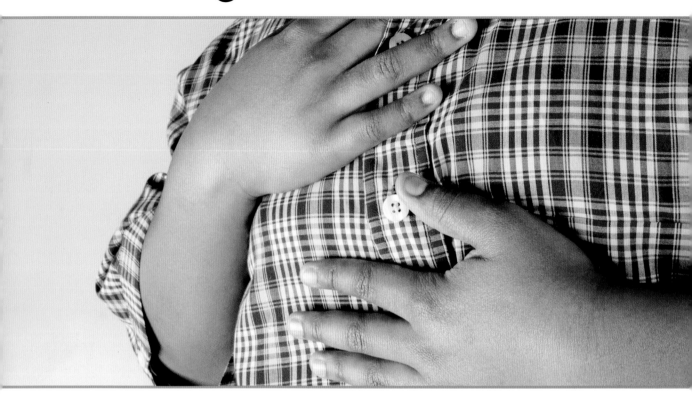

You can feel your lungs move.

You can feel your lungs breathe in and out.

Your lungs breathe in air.

Your need air to live.

Fast and Slow

When you are still your lungs breathe slowly.

When you run your lungs
breathe fast.

Staying Healthy

Smoking can hurt your lungs.

Exercise can help your lungs.

Quiz

Where in your body are your lungs?

Answer on page 24

Picture Glossary

air we need to breathe air in to stay alive. Air is all around us but we cannot see it.

breathe take in air

lungs parts of your body that help you breathe. You have two lungs inside your chest.

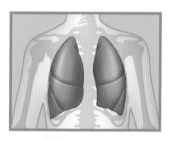

tube a long, thin pipe like a hose. Things can move through tubes because they have an empty space in the middle.

Index

Answer to quiz on page 22: Your lungs are in your chest.

Notes to parents and teachers

Before reading

Ask children to name the parts of their body they can see on the outside. Then ask them what parts of their body are inside. Make a list of them together and see if the children know what each body part does, for example, stomachs break down food. Discuss where their lungs are and ask if anyone knows what lungs do.

After reading

- Take the children outside and ask them to notice how they are breathing. Then tell them to run around for five minutes. When they stop, ask them to think again about how they are breathing. What do they notice?
- Talk to the children about how smoking can damage our lungs and other parts of our bodies. Discuss what they can do to help their lungs stay healthy.

24